HOW TO BE
NORMAL
IN
AUSTRALIA

HOW TO BE NORMAL IN AUSTRALIA

A PRACTICAL GUIDE TO THE UNCHARTED TERRITORY OF ANTIPODEAN RELATIONSHIPS

Robert Treborlang

Illustrations by Mark Knight

Major Mitchell Press

To Moi Moi's beauty and brilliant brain

First Published July 1987 by
Major Mitchell Press
P.O. Box 997, Potts Point, 2011.
Reprinted August 1987
Reprinted November 1987
Reprinted April 1988
Reprinted July 1989
Reprinted May 1990
Reprinted August 1996

Cover by Mark Knight
Book design by John Byrne
Typeset by Keyset Phototype, Sydney
Printed by McPherson's Printing Group

National Library of Australia

Cataloguing-in-Publication Data

Treborlang, Robert.
How to be Normal in Australia

ISBN 0 958770 8 0 8

1. National characteristics, Australian. 2. Australia—Social Life and
customs. I. Title.

Contents

Initiation

Just before lunch on a public holiday, I woke up in Australia. Having survived my first few months — learnt not to ask questions, never dress well and always look busy, I had at long last received an invitation to a genuine Australian barbecue. The sky was piercing blue, the air scorching hot. I felt like an explorer about to step into new uncharted territory.

My host welcomed me at the front door and quickly led me through the house to the backyard. People stood around in groups in a cafeteria-like atmosphere. The sun was at its zenith and meat was being thrown on the smoky grill.

"Help yourself," said my host.

I'd never before seen an Australian barbecue in action and felt excited. It was like finding out how the Royal Family behaved in private. Just what exactly happened there? What were Australians like away from the public eye?

It was only some hours later, that I began to realize that polite and apologetic, people spoke to each other no differently from those I had met in offices, factories and streets. There appeared to be an arm's length even among the closest relatives and friends.

When I discussed my observation with a few of the other guests, they advised me to have another drink.

At first I thought that everyone was tired from a week's hard work but after attending a great number of such events, I became aware that Australians were like this all the time. In fact, no one appeared to have any personal problems or worries. Unlike people in overseas societies. Australians just didn't seem to have the need to be too close to one another.

Could it be that they were a race apart? Maybe they were communicating in a different dimension.

I started to feel envious. I wanted to be like the people around me. Everybody acted so normal, so problem-free. I was like a visitor to an island paradise who longed to emulate the mystifying philosophy of the carefree locals.

But how?

Perhaps the key to everything was to create just the right distance between ourselves and others. Maybe the secret was to treat friends, family members and strangers all alike.

I set myself the task of finding out . . .

The National Etiquette

When unrestrained emotional Italians have a problem, they expect the whole world to take an interest, listen and help them solve it. Friends are selfishly contacted at two in the morning, hours are spent discussing the minutest details and litres of coffee and tears are poured out, while all manner of possible suggestions are put forward.

No Australian would stand for such behaviour.

In the United States, too, there are millions of brash, pushy and loud people running around with a variety of problems, complaining to family, friends, colleagues, psychiatrists, social counsellors, therapists, self-help organizations, positive thinking groups, or to anyone in subways and bars.

No Australian would stand for such behaviour either.

Australians are a polite and courteous people. Here it's considered bad manners to foist your problems onto others. You may be in the middle of a nervous breakdown, you may even have in-laws staying with you, but under no circumstances are you to admit to any difficulties.

"How's it going?"

"Great!"

"Are those your crutches?"

"Marvellous, aren't they?"

"What about the neck brace?"

"Brand new!"

While Australians have problems like everyone else, it is considered highly improper to voice these in intelligible exact terms. Polite Australians always talk about things that bother them with veiled cryptic comments. Well-bred people, they would never let on to what it is that's really wrong.

Under no condition are the issues that trouble you to be voiced in clear precise terms. Never actually refer to the problem itself. Always act as if your problem is something that's all over now and no longer of any consequence. Make it impossible for people to help you.

A German with matrimonial troubles, for example, will most likely take a swig of *schnapps,* turn to a friend and say: "I had an argument with Helga last night and she told me that if I didn't stop seeing other women and start coming home on time, she'd walk out on me."

This rude, obnoxious, over-precise way of talking about problems is simply not acceptable in Australia. An Australian in a similar predicament, after a long evening of inconsequential conversation with a friend, would remark:

"Jane's been strange lately."

"Oh, yeah?"

"She's been acting sort of funny."

"Hmmm."

"Makes one wonder . . ."

Another very important rule emerges here. Well-brought up friends in Australia know always to keep their distance and not get involved. The degree to which you can distance yourself from someone with a problem, in fact, and insist on not helping them solve it, is recognized as a measure of your good manners.

"It's up to you."

"I don't care either way."

"Whatever makes you happy."

Remember that should you, in a moment of weakness, take note of the problems of others or even offer to help them, there's a good chance that they'll shun you ever after for your tactless behaviour. You may know that the lives of Fiona, Gary or Greg are currently in a

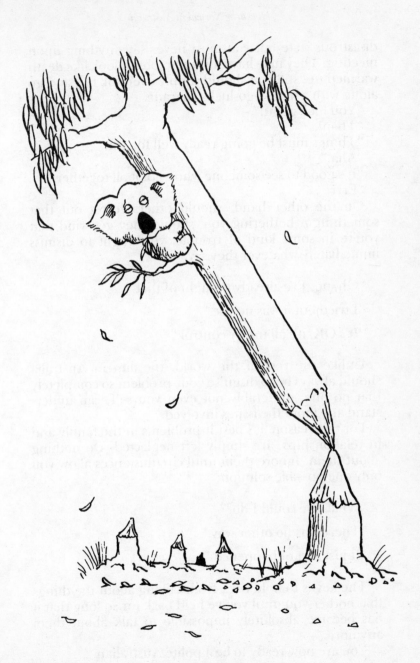

"It sort of just happened."

disastrous state but you must never say anything upon meeting. They may have lost their jobs or look like death warmed up, still you should simply overlook this and go along with a happy-go-lucky charade.

"You look great!"

"Thanks."

"Things must be going really well for you."

"Aha."

"It's good to see someone who's got it all together."

"Errr . . ."

On the other hand, should others ferret out that something *is* bothering you, should they get wind that you're in some kind of trouble, you ought to dismiss immediately whatever they say.

"Oh, no, I've already thought of that."

"I tried but it was no use."

"It's OK, it's all under control."

Unlike the rest of the world, the aim in Australia should always be to disguise your problem so completely that no one, preferably not even yourself, can understand any more the issues involved.

For this reason, it's best if problems in the family and in relationships, are simply left neglected. Do nothing about them. Ignore them until circumstances allow you only one possible solution:

"What else could I do?"

"There was no other way."

"It just sort of happened."

The key is to hold back from talking about the things that bother you until you've held back for so long that it has become absolutely impossible to talk about them anymore.

You are now ready to be a polite Australian.

The National Sport

In Italy the national sport is chasing the opposite sex; in Brazil, dabbling in *candomble* witchcraft; in Hungary, attempting suicide on quiet Sunday afternoons; in India, going on pilgrimage to remote and inaccessible temples; in the Soviet Union, dodging the secret police.

In Australia the national sport is splitting-the-bill.

Unknown in most other countries, splitting-the-bill is as uniquely Australian as the great rock of Uluru or the small perforations in Sao biscuits. Practised in the nation's restaurants, coffee lounges and hotels by people of all ages and backgrounds, bill-splitting is the embodiment of the Australian's personal commitment to fair play.

"Let me take care of this."

"Don't be silly."

"Ah, thanks."

"No, no, we'll split the bill."

The Chinese, by contrast, brought up under oligarchic regimes, do not accept the division of any restaurant account. Among them it is always the eldest at the table or the person responsible for the inviting, who does the paying. The Greeks too, warped by centuries of Turkish oppression, refute bill-splitting, and will fight to the last for the right to settle the entire tab.

Australians, unaware of their global uniqueness in this field, split bills on every conceivable occasion and as often as possible. With the single-minded devotion of those who know of no alternatives, they take the entire process rather seriously and practise with the fervour of devoted afficionados.

Like all deeply rooted indigenous sports, splitting-the-bill has strict rules which Australians learn from early childhood.

"I'm telling you, I didn't have the garlic bread!"

If you happen to come from an alien background, you might do well to practise at home and in small groups, until you're proficient enough to try it out in public.

There are several steps to follow:

1 Six good friends meet and decide to have a meal at an ethnic restaurant. All evening they remark how nice the place is, how good the food is and how cheap it is. Finally the bill arrives.

2 The bill is passed around and everyone studies the addition as if memorising it. No conversation takes place while this ritual occurs. Everyone is intent on the final outcome. Eventually a voice is heard to say:

"Twenty-two dollars each."*

3 You can be sure there's a few startled reactions:
   "I didn't eat the garlic bread."
   "But you had the mineral water."
   "I didn't have a first course."
   "You had some of my pancakes."
   "But not the cucumber salad."
   "*I* certainly didn't order it."

4 Details sorted out, the friends reach into their pockets and put some money on the plate. *Invariably the total comes to the wrong amount.*
   "It's four dollars short!"
   "It wasn't me."
   "Me neither."
   "Not me."
   "And I haven't got my change yet."

Silence.

"We'll have to put in an extra 80 cents each."

5 Everyone throws down some coins and scurries away in a bad mood, before the waiter notices that they've left no tip.

---

* *One can always tell well-bred Australians from the speed with which they work out their share of a bill.*

How to avoid people

Australians are a cordial and friendly people who seem to more than welcome you into their midst. This natural openness should not be abused, however, and you'd be well-advised to practise the restraint Australians clearly expect and deserve.

On trains and buses

Always sit on your own, as far away as possible from other passengers. This will show that you are both serious and self contained. Do not stare about you, fidget or hum in the manner of many overseas travellers. It's best to gaze at some unseen, inner landscape, as if in a trance.

Only when the entire bus or carriage is filled in this way is it permissible to sit next to others. You may now take a seat next to a stranger, but only with the utmost reserve and nervous uncertainty. *Ensure that no part of your body or clothing touches theirs.* Pick passengers not out of personal preference but because:

(a) they seem the least offensive; or

(b) they look as if they're about to hop off.

Standing in queues

Do not attempt to engage anyone in conversation while queueing up at a bank, a government office or some

When all the seats are taken.

other public place. It might be acceptable to launch into a discussion with perfect strangers in Zagreb or Naples; many insecure Europeans, who've never met before, often end up having drinks together or beginning life-long friendships, simply through asking each other the time.

Australians, self-assured inhabitants of the world's largest isle, have no such immature habits and feel no need to communicate with strangers. On the contrary, since being singled out makes them feel ridiculous, Australians think it rather important to put unknown persons in their place and force them to realise that it is just what they ought to remain — unknown.

In the street

Should others approach *you,* the situation could be equally tricky. You're standing on a street corner, for example, with four of your girlfriends or mates. A well-dressed stranger with an open face walks up to you, wanting some information.

What are you to do?

1 Look quizzically with a frowning stare at your four friends who, all being Australian, will simultaneously return the same look to you. This long silent pause is essential to put the friendly stranger ill at ease.

2 Issue a series of non-lexical sounds as slowly as possible. "Um...gee...aaah...yeah..."

3 Pass the responsibility on to the person next to you: "Err...Ron, you'd know something about that..." (This well-rehearsed exchange is constantly practised in the Australian home, where Mum and Dad are always "passing the buck" to each other.)

4 Be very careful not to return the stranger's friendliness as that could embarrass your

Australian friends. The conversation, already staggering, should now collapse completely.

Remember that Australians in their childhood are told to beware of people, never to talk to anybody with too friendly a smile on their face, and to ignore those who wish to engage them in conversation. Sure, you might miss out on a few boiled lollies, but think of the successful way you can overcome some of the greatest perils of growing up:

(a) finding out new information;
(b) making new friends;
(c) learning to cope with life through spontaneity and charm.

Always be sorry

Parents in Germany constantly encourage offspring to be thorough in everything they do. In the United States, kids are prodded to save whatever money they earn. In Japan, infants are urged to become loyal and hardworking. In Australia much of the time and energy spent on education goes into teaching children the importance of being sorry.

"Say you're sorry!"

"And what do we say now?"

"You better apologize or else!"

One can tell, in fact, sophisticated and well-brought-up Australians from the frequency with which they say they're sorry.

"I'm awfully sorry but..."

"I hope you don't mind that..."

"I regret to have to do this, however..."

In France, birthplace of courtly manners, should someone step on your foot it is socially quite acceptable to retort with something like: "Get off my bloody foot!" Such a statement in Australia just wouldn't be considered good enough. Properly educated apologetic Australians, if they say anything at all, would be expected to remark:

"I'm sorry to bother you and I hope I'm not too much

21

trouble but could you move your foot a little either way because somehow mine seems to have got caught under yours."

Then, for good measure, you could also add (again): "I really *am* sorry."

In this country you should never miss an opportunity to apologize. Do it under every possible pretext and with friends and strangers alike. You must say you're sorry especially: if you are right; if you think you might be right; if others agree that you're right; if you tell someone that you like them; if you're suspected of having made a mistake; if someone else makes a mistake; if you're getting drunk and falling over; if you don't happen to drink at all; if you happen to disagree with someone; if they disagree with you; if you are about to express an opinion; if you lose at a game; if you win at a game; if you haven't apologized for a while.

On arrival at an Australian home it's a good idea to start apologizing the moment you come in through the door. *Being on time* is a good excuse, i.e.: "I'm sorry to be so punctual." On being offered a drink you must excuse yourself for proving a bother, or better even, for actually being thirsty. It's advisable to throw in a few random apologies to keep the conversation going when sitting down, such as: "I'm sorry, have I sat on the wrong chair?"

It's also good form to be sorry for having burped. Even if it's impossible for other people to have heard it, you must bring your hand up to your mouth and stop all conversation with a loud: "I'm terribly sorry, it's awfully rude of me." In France and Germany, indeed, you might be thought gauche if you made such a statement. In Australia a bold apology for even the quietest little burp is considered the quintessence of courtly behaviour and your hosts will rush to have you over again.

Like religion, being sorry is something in which everyone must participate — a sort of chain reaction without end in sight. For example, it's important once someone apologizes to immediately apologize back.

"*I'm sorry to bother you and I hope I'm not too much trouble but could you move your foot a little either way because somehow mine seems to have got caught under yours.*"

"I'm sorry I took longer than I thought."

"Oh, I'm sorry, I should've realized."

"It's my fault and I'm sorry I didn't ring."

"I'm sorry then to put you to all this trouble."

"Oh no, I'm the one sorry for the inconvenience."

"No, no, it was definately my fault. So sorry."

Whatever you do, don't break the chain as it is considered both rude and dangerous. Unreassured apologetic Australians may even get aggressive. Australians who are not allowed to complete their apology become wild creatures indeed.

"I hope you'll forgive me for being late."

"OK."

"I'm sorry but it wasn't my fault."

"Good."

"I'll make sure it won't happen again."

"Fine."

"I said I'm sorry."

"I know."

"You don't believe me."

"I do."

"Listen, I can't do more than apologize."

"I understand."

"Well, if you're going to take that attitude, I'm sorry, but I'll have to leave."

Due to all these uses of the word "sorry", its actual meaning has somewhat changed. You must, therefore, *not* say sorry under the following circumstances: if you *know* you're in the wrong; if you know you've hurt someone's feelings; if you've made a mistake; when talking to somebody who has recently suffered a bereavement.

In these situations the best line is always: "I just don't know what to say."

Grimacing for beginners

Try as you may to absorb local customs, imitate slang or penetrate Australia's national psyche, you will never be considered normal until you *look right* — until you look at ease in this unique environment. And what makes Australians *look right* are the faces they pull.

An honest Australian farmer who makes an impassioned speech on behalf of the country's struggling wheat growers, might just escape being labelled a "whinger". A mediocre actor in a corporate TV commercial, however, has only to jerk his neck and twitch the corner of his mouth and he'll be said to embody the indomitable fighting spirit of Australia.

Clearly, a grimace is worth a thousand words.

Here then are a variety of scowls, contortions and grins that you should learn to disport on various appropriate occasions:

Type one: "Uh-uh."

The most popular way to start really pulling faces is when somebody suddenly becomes passionate about a particular subject. This usually happens when you're in a group.

In Israel or Greece impassioned views would set the scene for an interesting discussion, but in Australia you and your friends must start to eye one another nervously, while frowning heavily with a series of painful

25

mouth contortions, to indicate a speaker who has gone off the rails.

If this doesn't work, re-form the party in such a way that the speaker is excluded. It's sure to achieve the desired results — as he is now talking to himself, while the rest of you telegraph to each other his obvious mental disturbance with a series of repetitive exaggerated grimaces.

Type two: "Oh-oh."

You've been invited to dinner. An attractive guest has started to gaze in your direction. Are you being asked to pass the salt? Is it someone next to you? Check. Eventually, you may have to accept the reality of the situation — someone is trying to flirt with you. What are you to do?

If you're a woman, compress neck, flare nostrils, tighten lips and show a congested expression. If you're a man, stiffen your face, look rigid and gaze intently just past the person who likes you. In France or Hungary, being admired makes people talkative and charming; in Australia if you're liked, wear a strict mask.

Type three: The Migraine Squint.

Here's a general grimace for when you're out and about.

The eyes are narrowed to accentuate the crows feet, the eyebrows are jammed into a straight line and the neck is locked into an angular position, allowing no sideward head-movement whatever.

Definitely to be worn in public places, this migraine-like-squint will give you the ability to walk down the street and not see anything, while warning people, at the same time to stay away from you.

Type four: Super-glue.

You're at a gathering. There's a rumour that someone

Keeping people at bay in public.

"Oh-oh. Must be careful. Someone over there likes me."

The only way to get into the papers.

"Uh-uh. They're getting passionate about ideas."

from a newspaper or a magazine has been spotted wandering with a camera among the crowd. It could be anybody. What can you do?

Start grinning.

Raise eyebrows to suggest naivete. Draw mouth-muscles right back. Bare teeth to the gums. Keep smile and eyes immobile as if they had been super-glued onto your face. Behave as in a trance.

In Australia, without the super-glue look they'll never print your photo in the papers.

Mother's Day

March the 8th throughout the world is "Women's Day". On this date, all men from young to old, give flowers, gifts and special dinners to the females in their lives, in appreciation of feminine attributes and achievements. On Women's Day the entire female sex is celebrated.

Such a manifestation of feeling has been found to be insufficient in this country. While every Australian's mother is undoubtedly a female, lumping her together with the rest of the world simply did not seem fair, seeing that her roles and responsibilities are so much greater.

To begin with, Australian mothers allow their children a vast deal of freedom and youngsters grow up with hardly any restraints. It is rare to see limitations imposed even upon the youngest of infants. Children are permitted to develop naturally and unencumbered from birth, according to the best pioneering traditions. There *are*, however, a few limitations which even the most liberal-minded mother must observe, if her offspring are to fit into this society.

Helpful

All curiosity manifested by children for objects or ideas, ought to be countered and rebuked with a healthy:

"Don't you touch anything!"

The Mother in Irons.

"Don't be a sticky beak!"

"It's none of your business!"

Should any adult relative or friend address your children directly, a mother must always make a point of jumping in and answering for the kids:

"Bianca doesn't know."

"Trent is too young to understand."

"Jane is not feeling well today."

Embarrassing displays of affection on the part of the children for other people, ought to be prevented at all costs with a stern:

"Don't bother Uncle Bill!"

"Leave Aunty Violet alone!"

"Stop being a nuisance!"

Practical

Overseas mothers waste a lot of their children's time with pointless reminiscences, idle dreams, silly pranks and foolish romantic stories. Australia must be the only country in the world where a mother's conversation is entirely instructional, as she is determined to improve her children at every chance she gets.

"Tidy your room."

"Hang up your clothes."

"Rinse your plate."

Patient

Only Australian mothers know how hard it is to teach kids the meaning of patience. Techniques differ from household to household, but making children wait for their nourishment is perhaps still the most effective.

The instant a child asks to be fed or arrives home hungry and expecting alimentation, it is a mother's duty to reply with a clear:

"Wait a minute!"

"I'm busy!"

"I've only got one pair of hands."

It's advisable to keep the kids waiting for anything from twenty minutes to an entire afternoon. You certainly shouldn't just dish out the food as youngsters might start taking it for granted. The advantage is that it prepares them for life in Australia, where things always take a little longer than everyone thinks.

In recognition of these and many other admirable attributes, Australians have set aside the second Sunday in each May to celebrate with a great deal of devotion mothers right across the country.

On this day from early morning everyone in the family is busy preparing for the festivities. The men fight over who'll make the toast, the girls bring flowers and chocolates. Older children make an effort to turn up. They might take you out for a meal, or just give you nylon brunchcoats, cordless irons, fluffy pink slippers, tools to turn carrots into flowers, or maybe even a nonstick skillet.

Never appear worried

To be normal in Australia you must never appear to worry about anything. Jovial and carefree, Australians pride themselves in being able to remain optimistic even in the face of the greatest adversity.

It may be acceptable to worry in Greece, Italy, or Yugoslavia. Nobody disputes the state of pessimism that rides roughshod over those lands. But in Australia, a young and vital nation, it is your duty to be nonchalant at all times. Everyone must deny any concern or emotional involvement, no matter what the situation.

"It's got nothing to do with me."

"I can't be bothered."

"Things always sort themselves out."

This attitude should be carried into all walks of life, especially road accidents. The instant you see one, rush over with the greatest possible speed, join the already growing crowd of idle observers, force your way to the front and make your optimistic views clearly known.

"He'll be right."

"I've seen much worse."

"It's only a surface wound."

"Doctors can do wonders these days."

"Reckon they'll have those legs sewn back in no

"A bit of physio and he'll be up and running."

time at all."

"A bit of physio and he'll be up and running."

"You hear that, mate? Mate? Mate?"

Take care, however. Under no condition are you to touch, help or move the victim, since that is the job of the proper authorities (anyone with a badge). Besides, should you do the wrong thing, you'll probably end up getting sued.

Your job is merely to be positive and reassuring.

There *are*, of course, the occasional pessimistic on-lookers with a compulsion to rush in, attend to the victim and race him or her to medical attention under their own steam. It goes without saying that these are negative thinking individuals who always assume the worst. Luckily their numbers are fast dwindling due to the realisation that too much initiative is really un-Australian.

Being cheery and worry-free is one thing, of course. Accusing others of worrying is another. Be careful never to say "You look worried, mate", or "Stop worrying" to an Australian, because that's how you start an argument.

"Frankly, I wouldn't worry."

"Who's worried?"

"Some people worry a lot."

"Not me, I never worry."

"I certainly don't."

"Well, I don't either."

"Why should I worry?"

"There's nothing to worry about."

In fact, saying "you look worried" to someone in Australia is tantamount to perpetrating a personal attack on them. By ascribing to people as much as a hint of worry, you've virtually accused them of:

(a) not being able to cope

(b) having failed the Australian jollity test

(c) being in need of psychiatric counselling

Should someone accuse *you* of being worried, or worse still, of *looking* worried, it's vital to demonstrate right away that you're nothing of the sort:

1 Scowl affronted as if they had said that your breath smells.

2 Talk about all the other people you know who have *real* worries — dob in everybody you can.

3 Sink low in your seat as if you're about to nod off, to show how relaxed you are.

Always project a worry-free image.* Act as if concern is the furthest thought from your mind. In fact, the worse things are, the more light-hearted you ought to appear.

Remember, in Australia, the only worrying you should do is never to appear worried.

It's alright, however, to worry about numbers, i.e.:
"Did I drink 4 or 5 beers at lunchtime?"
"Will I back the 3rd in the 4th at Doomben?"
"I wonder which of the 6 plugs is misfiring?"

How to be passive

Whilst in Europe, Asia and America men without initiative might be shunned, avoided or even ostracized, in Australia this quality is actively sought out, recognized and encouraged by every ' sensitive and romantic woman.

What elegance and *savoir faire* do for French girls, or bareback yak hunting does for Tibetan beauties, showing lack of initiative does to the Australian female.

To Europeans, indeed, the attraction Australian women feel for men who sit in corners all night, staring at their nails, or who gaze wistfully at wallpaper patterns, may seem slightly eccentric. To the Japanese the penchant of the Australian female for making the first move towards a relationship might even seem pushy. To South Americans, not unexpectedly, the Australian male's habit of waiting to be spoken to would seem rather unexciting.

Australian males, of course, know better. They understand only too well that the less energy they expand and the more passive they behave, the greater their chances of being picked up. They know that women have to be allowed to take the initiative, otherwise things would never get anywhere. After all, there's nothing Australian females suspect more than a man going out of his way to make an impression.

"He likes you."

"He's a creep."

"What's he done?"

"Keeps on telling me how much he likes me."

I discovered the importance of acting passive at my very first Australian party. Around midnight I began to notice that guys who, till then, had sat around in corners and never paid the slightest attention to anyone or anything all night, were now approached by girls who had spent the whole time chatting to each other.

"You're very quiet."

"I'm alright."

"You don't seem to be enjoying yourself."

"I'm not a party person."

"Neither am I really."

"I like to get to know people one at a time."

"Why don't we go outside then?"

"Alright."

I realised that Australian women were strong-minded, proud individuals who would hate the idea of someone deliberately setting out to seduce them. A man may entertain desires, he may even have designs, but they should not be revealed under any circumstances.

"What shall we do?"

"Up to you."

"A drive?"

"I don't mind."

"Where to?"

"I'm easy."

Since the aim is to protect the woman from feeling that advantage is being taken of her, and as even the most minimal difference of opinion could land you in trouble, further conversations ought to be limited to a few neutral topics. Any of the following will do:

- the trade-in value of cars

- the pros and cons of various alarm systems

- what sandwiches you have for lunch

- problems of people she's never met

Equally important is to be passive in a relationship. Should someone telephone, for instance, to invite the

How to be passive.

two of you, care must be taken not to show too independent a spirit.

"What are you doing next Saturday?"

"I'm not sure."

"Would you like to come to a party?"

"Wait till I ask Fiona."

In Germany or Russia it may be acceptable for a man to reply promptly "Yes" to an invitation. In Australia, however, it is the woman's prerogative only to pick up the phone and accept with a cheery:

"We'd love to come."

Failure to comply with the simple rules of passivity could rapidly escalate into circumstances beyond anyone's control.

"What did you do that for?"

"What's that?"

"Saturday was going to be my quiet night."

"I just thought..."

"Well, you can go on your own."

It's best not to reply. Sit on the edge of a chair or sofa and gaze crestfallen at the floor, until your partner relents.

And if you're passive enough, they will.

Why kissing always means "yes"

It's all very well for Italians or South Americans to kiss at the slightest pretext — flirtatious people by nature, for them kissing is a shallow affair. Many may even do it with people on whom they have absolutely no designs.

Australians, highly moral and honourable by contrast, will kiss for one purpose and one purpose only.

In Europe when two people get to kiss each other, they often perform the act in a passionate though not overly optimistic manner. Europeans as a rule kiss purely for pleasure, often using it to avoid deeper, more intimate commitments.

In Australia once you've kissed there's no turning back. Australians kiss to let you know that they're ready. Like now.

"Mmmm. That was nice."

"Yeah"

"Something just clicked."

"Sure did."

"Wait till I lock the door."

Kissing is the key ritual of an otherwise straightforward operation. Australians are meticulous about kissing and have made it the cornerstone of sex.

"Kiss me again."

"No."

"Why?"

"Let's make love instead."

After all, if you are going to go to all the trouble and

actually invade someone's personal space, you might as well go all the way.

Many people from overseas, after making initial contact with Australians and kissing them quite passionately, think nothing more of it. On the following occasion, wishing to pick up where they left off, these folk are shocked to find that they no longer arouse the same degree of interest as before.

"What's wrong?"

"Nothing."

"Then kiss me."

"What's the point?"

"I like you!"

"You sure didn't show it last time."

The most popular and successful lovers in Australia know to hold back to the last moment and not to waste their kisses on hellos or goodbyes. They know only too well that kissing must be reserved for the following occasions:

(a) as an indication of readiness;

(b) as a signal that the congress is over; and

(c) when you're drunk.

A successful romantic evening in Australia consists of not kissing on meeting, absolutely not touching during dinner, major physical reticence on the way home, total abstinence while sitting around before the TV set, not even a hint of physical closeness while you're having that last nightcap. Then, just as you are about to say goodbye and both are wondering whether perhaps the other one is not a bit funny, one all-exploding kiss must come as a complete and instant outpouring of tension.

Your highly reticent and moral Australian is now ready.

A modest observation

Men in Australia become homosexual if they like women and heterosexual if they don't.

This transcendental truth came to me early on when I made the acquaintance of a beautiful Australian girl. No sooner were we introduced, than she began to treat me like an old friend. She rewarded my compliments with little hugs, laughed at my travel adventures and in general acted wonderfully relaxed.

At the end of the evening I took her home. Seated on her sofa, close to each other, we continued telling amusing stories over a cup of coffee. Suddenly as she brushed close to me, I leaned forward and kissed the girl on the mouth. She tensed up, became stiff and pressed herself against the far edge of the sofa.

"What's wrong?" I said.

"I thought you were homosexual," she told me.

"How come?"

"You're too friendly to be straight."

"But you were friendly too!" I exclaimed.

"Because I thought you were gay!"

From that moment on the atmosphere changed dramatically.

The conversation was no longer easy-going and the girl behaved with an odd formality. No matter how affectionately I treated her, she responded tautly and spoke with long awkward pauses.

"Sure you aren't homosexual?" she asked again.

"Of course not."

Heterosexual.

"Only gay men act so relaxed with women here."

"Then how do Australian heterosexual men act?" I asked.

"*Nor*mal," she said.

After much trial and error, I discovered over the next few months that only when I too tensed up, acted gruff and spoke with long awkward pauses, did Australian women seem to take my advances seriously and accept me as a potential romantic partner.

I had stumbled upon the Australian *heterosexual mode* and uncovered two very important basic rules:

1 Gay men in Australia behave towards women with the same relaxed, easy-going attitude that heterosexual men manifest towards women in Europe. Brought up by righteous-minded mothers and aunts, homosexuals here have a deep respect for females and would rather regard other men only as sex objects. By contrast, and in order to be identified as heterosexuals, straight men in Australia have to act surly, tense and uneasy with women, as if they didn't like them at all. They must also look ready to bolt at any moment and run back to their mates.

Homosexual.

2 Gay men in Australia, when visiting their women friends, bring flowers, boxes of chocolates or champagne, much like straight men do in Europe. They are also the ones who entertain the women with amusing stories and flattering compliments at parties and in public places. Heterosexual Australian men, on the other hand, wanting to be recognised as such, have no choice but to slouch in corners and grunt into their drinks. Since they also consider taking presents when visiting rather cissy, straight men prefer just to bring themselves.

Sex by attrition

When Iraq and Iran went to war the whole world expected a quick end to the conflict. Instead the two countries settled down to a long-winded struggle with the aim of wearing down each other's resistance.

It's what is called a war of attrition.

If you want to be successful with the opposite sex in Australia, you must learn the art of attrition, as courtship Down-under is run along much the same lines.

Australians, you see, are independent and proud beings who consider that any admission of desire shows a demeaning lack of character. One may have urges, one may even entertain certain designs, but these should not be revealed under any circumstances. On the contrary, all references to real intentions ought to bring out a hot denial:

"I think you've got the wrong idea about me."

"I'm just not like that."

"It was the last thing on my mind."

Half-hearted excuses like "What's wrong with that?" and "Haven't had it for weeks" simply won't do. Even the slightest admission of desire can lead to untold complications and risks being seen like trying to extract sex from the other person.

"You're not really a bad sort."

"Thanks."

"I reckon you look a bit of all right."

"Oh yeah?"

"So, what shall we do now?"

"Actually I quite like you."

"I knew you'd turn out to be a creep."

It may be admissible for a Frenchman to sight a pretty girl in Montmartre, share a quick lunch with her and then, after declaring his intentions, end up having a siesta together an hour later. In Australia this kind of spontaneity is frowned upon and is seen in the same light as queue-jumping.

Australians are a well-brought-up moral nation who've learnt since childhood that you've got to take the bad with the good. After all, one can't just go from soup to dessert. And one certainly couldn't have sweets on its own.

"Finish your vegetables."

"But I don't want to!"

"Finish them!"

"Can't I just have dessert?"

"You'll eat your greens or go without!"

Successful Australian lovers, therefore, go out together for drinks, eat something, then walk around a bit, have a few more drinks, go to a movie, drive back to either one's place, sit around, play some records, snack, watch the late news, have another drink, sit around some more or read the papers and then, when they run out of all other possibilities, when there is absolutely nothing left to do, they go to bed.

It's sex by attrition.

How to become respectable

To earn people's respect in England you'd do well to marry into a family with a long lineage. In an Eastern Bloc country it's best to become involved in the Communist Party. Respect in most Arab countries is earned by praying in a mosque five times a day. If you want to be respected in Australia, however, you must become a heavy and committed gambler.

Australians have a great admiration for gamblers and see them as embodiments of the national ethos — something like the way the Swiss regard their more established bankers.

Unimaginative Europeans, brought up to regard gambling as wasteful, fail to see how risking a large percentage of one's weekly income on a horse running 3000 kms away, can be an expression of one's respectability. Australians, of course, know better. They realize that more than a flag, an anthem or a coast to coast highway, a nation gambling as one will always be united against all odds.

True, every country has its pockets of gambling, but they are regarded merely as an aberration, as something to be done on the sly, in one's spare time and with the connivance of a few shady individuals. No German or Italian politician would dream of flaunting their gambling habits to family, colleagues or constituents. Even in an amoral country like France gambling is seen as something one performs on the quiet, a habit some-

"I got my owner an Order of Australia. What did you get yours?"

where between picking one's nose and snatching hand-bags on the subway.

Australians were the first nation to break through these old-world taboos. Far from apologising for it, they've made gambling the cornerstone of their nation-hood and use it the way Popes used religion to unite medieval Europe. An intricate network covers the country for this purpose:

Racecourses, dog tracks, poker machines, lottery agencies, two-up schools, TAB offices, SP shops, bingo houses, trotting meets, stock exchanges, futures markets, art-union mailouts, church raffles, write-in competitions, lotto promotions, luxury casinos, golden caskets, instant prizes, soccer pools, cockroach races and earth-worm tournaments.

You may hear in fact mysterious incantations wherever you go:

"Eleven and twenty-five always come up together."

"The third in the fourth looks good."

"I was told I'd only get four to seven on the red in the second but I got on at four to five."

In Europe if you can identify every one of Mozart's symphonies, people will say about you "That person is cultured." Do the same thing in Australia and you'll be called a show-off. Name, however, every horse and rider who's won the Melbourne Cup since 1861 and you will be regarded with great respect.

Talking about race-horses or dogs is never showing off. You are admired as someone worthwhile. It's OK to be interested even in something like computers as long as you intend to use it for working out winners at the track or lucky Lotto numbers.

Men and women who back in Budapest, Zurich or Vienna would have never dreamt of gambling 5 dinars of their hard earned money, and whose parents would have turned white at the thought of their children wasting their wages, in Australia soon shed all inhibitions and devote many waking hours to this new fount of respectability.

It's not as if they're gambling — they're simply trying to gain acceptance. Accountants, lawyers, general practitioners, all do it, purely to be sociable and earn the respect of their clients, of course. Most of the clients are at the races, anyway.

In other countries unenlightened parents are horrified if their children gamble. In Australia, parents keen to see their kids grow up respected members of the community, encourage gambling from an early age.

"Don't waste your money, Bev! Better buy Lotto!"

"Grandpa reckons Concerto is set to win."

"I bought everyone scratchies for Christmas but gave Mum an Opera House and Dad a Systems Seven."

It's important, therefore, to train children from an early age to buy lotteries for birthdays, hold intra-family Melbourne Cup sweeps, organize clan nights at the pokies, watch Lotto results gathered around the telly, and to put into practice the wise old dictum: *the family that bets together, gets together.*

The Australian Wedding

The world is familiar with the colourful traditions of Jewish and Greek weddings. Glasses and plates are broken, elaborate rituals accompany every word and there's a great deal of chanting. Not to be outdone, Australians too have devised a complex wedding ritual, as rich in meaning and prescribed behaviour as anything you'll find among the Berbers of the Atlas Mountains or the Uzbeks of Tadjikistan.

Traditionally, each aspect of an Australian wedding constitutes a different struggle. Each planned stage leading up to the actual tying of the matrimonial knot must be the source of acrimonious fights between both bride and groom and their respective anxious families.

"I'm not having Peter as the best man."

"But he's my brother!"

"He's an airline steward!"

"Mum and Dad will be disappointed."

"What about *my* Mum and Dad?"

"They hate me anyway!"

"Because you won't be nice to them!"

As this is a frontier country with a strong pioneering background, such arguments are symbolic representations of the fighting spirit that typifies the Australian way of life.

Every step of the preparations, the date, the venue, the guest list, the presents, the food, the wine list, height of the wedding cake, who should be bridesmaid, who should be best man, what the weather's going to be like, why the wedding should be held in the first place, ought therefore to be the source of a new conflict.

Make sure the bride and groom have their own chance to be directly involved in the conflict every step of the way.

The guest list

Start by disagreeing on the number of guests to be invited. If one wants an intimate ceremony, declare that it's only out of meanness. If the wedding is planned for oodles of people, object to it on the grounds that it voids the intimate sense of marriage.

Neither side ought to like the other one's relatives or friends. Deprecate everyone suggested for invitation on the basis of job, manners, religion, or of what they said back at the engagement party. Threaten to call the whole thing off if the Lismore branch is coming.

The venue

If the other party wants the wedding at home, suggest an expensive hotel. Should they opt for the local RSL Club insist on a lavish restaurant. Argue for several weeks over the issue. Phone up and leave disturbing messages for one another. In the end settle on an asbestos lined community hall down the road, which though too narrow and too dark, is the only venue available for the set date.

The band

If the opposite side demand "young" music, put your foot down and make it clear that a wedding's not a wedding without a traditional band. If the foe wants mushy music to please the older generation, press for a modern raucous pop group.

Fight up to the last minute then hire a makeshift three piece orchestra, or four relatives, or a gaggle of professional musicians who've never played together before. Ensure there is a "singing" drunken uncle close on hand who can embarrass half the hall and anger the rest.

The food

For a REAL Australian wedding the fare has to be awful. This shouldn't be difficult to achieve once everyone agrees to disagree over the culinary details.

If the groom's crowd want everything catered, insist on the necessity of having home cooked food. Explain that you couldn't possibly disappoint Aunt Dot whose specialty is asparagus rolled in crustless bread with a toothpick through it. Nor can you let down Cousin Joyce who does wonders with pineapple rings and apple-pie-a-la-mode.*

If the bride's folks *do* decide to have the wedding lavishly catered, try to squeeze in as many of the groom's family and friends into the reception as you can. Point out that they *are* all your best mates and that they *did* invite you to *their* weddings. If this doesn't work, make a long list of allergy sufferers in the family who will need specially prepared meals.

Make sure you don't serve anchovies or anything smelly.

The drinks

The bride's kin ought to demand sophisticated drinks to go with the lovely dishes. This should cause a lot of trouble because drinks, traditionally, end up costing more than the food.

The groom's side, on the other hand, should announce loud and clear that since the bride's lot are just a bunch of drunkards, beer and extra-sweet sparkling wine will do just nicely.

---

* *A la mode in Australia usually means with a dob of aerosol whipped cream.*

Visions in fruitcake.

In revenge, the bride's relations can always make sure that the beer-cooling Temprite on the keg does not work properly, and that the carpet (or lawn) gets covered in a nice thick layer of froth.*

The cake

The *pièce de résistance*, of course.

It's never nice. Bake it well in advance to ensure just the right sort of dryness. This is a wonderful opportunity for future in-laws to join in a lively slanging match.

"Looks too rich for me."

"It's not *very* moist."

"If only they used my recipe."

"What a disappointment!"

"It's what comes from skimping."

All guests can now contribute by making snide remarks. Clan barriers break down and in matters of resentment it's everyone for themselves. Remember that the aim is to give the young couple a foretaste of the fighting spirit that has made Australia what she is today.

"You'd think they'd go to more trouble."

"He never even said thank you."

"Fancy seating me with that lot."

"I knew I spent too much on the present."

"I thought she'd end up with better than him."

And that classic of Australian classics:

"They've left us with all the mess!"

* *Known as "Tampering with the Temprite".*

Three games for beginners

Here are three amusing and very effective techniques for maintaining the optimum level of necessary tension with a partner, should you end up in an antipodean relationship.

Doesn't Matter

Whenever your partner comes into the house or you meet up somewhere, just stare into thin air with a vague expression. It is immensely satisfying to see them squirm as they try to find out what's wrong.

"You look upset."

"No, I don't."

"What did I do?"

"Forget it."

"I want to know."

"It doesn't matter."

This dialogue may be kept going until you get bored or your partner reaches breaking point.

Someone Saw You

If there's the occasional relaxed moment, never wait for it to be over. If you speak quietly and with good timing — and in Australia such timings are learnt from early childhood — the atmosphere will be instantly charged with tension and guilt.

"Someone saw you the other day."

"Really? Where?"

"They wouldn't say."

"Who was it?"
"I better not tell you."
"Why not?"
"You wouldn't like what they said."
"Why? What did they say? Tell me!"
"No, I better not."

This can go on for ever and is especially entertaining when you've made the whole thing up.

Us Really

Should your partner seem a little too happy or carefree, throw your head back, sigh, shut your eyes and tighten your lips.

"What's wrong?"
"I was just thinking."
"What about?"
"Us, really."
"What about us?"
"You wouldn't understand."

It is highly gratifying to see them tense up and start to worry. There's also a good chance they'll eventually develop an ulcer.

Bringing down children

Some countries, like Italy and France, hold to the belief that children can be *born* with special talents or aptitudes. In Russia and Japan it is believed that children *trained* from a tender age will show marvellous abilities. Australians, imbued as they are with the spirit of fairness, hold both these views to be untrue. In Australia, it is believed that not only are children all born the same, but that they must also be actively discouraged from becoming in any way different, more capable or better than their peers.

While overseas the aim is to bring children up, in Australia the idea is to bring them down.

The process has a few basic steps.

1 Childhood ought to consist of a series of "don'ts", uttered clearly and with dramatic authority from early infancy*. Under ideal conditions, "don't" should be the very first word a baby hears. The purpose is to impart on the child a vague feeling of guilt for every one of its actions, by never explaining what it is that's wrong.

2 If children show a natural passion for playing the piano, writing poems or leaping over tall fences, it's important to force them to spend as much time and

* *It's actually the middle classes who say "don't" to children. The upper classes prefer to say "do", i.e.:*
  - *Don't bother me! (middle class)*
  - *Do sit still! (upper class)*
  - *Don't touch anything on the shelves! (middle class)*
  - *Do help mummy with the shopping! (shopping class)*

"He's never gonna play for Australia."

energy as possible away from the things they're good at or have a talent for, in the hope that they'll lose interest or become too discouraged to go on.

"What are you up to?"
"Practising."
"What, again?"
"I'm sorry."
"You'd be better off doing something else."

Should they persist in doing things they're talented at, keep pointing out all the difficulties that lie ahead. Advise them to get involved with backyard cricket, pinball machines or the local pool instead. Explain that by being good just at the one thing will make them boring and unpopular with friends.

3 No one quite understands why some Australian children are born with a competitive spirit. Often terribly normal families bring forth kids who want to succeed in life for no explainable reason. Baffled parents have been urging the Government to study the problem for years. The affliction strikes at random and blights the unlikeliest youngsters. You may care to try the following popular remedies:
(a) Don't put any energy into developing the children;
(b) Keep them in a learn-free cocoon for as long as possible;
(c) Make certain they grow up no better than yourself — the motto here ought to be: *I want my children to have all the things I've had, but no more.*

4 Most importantly don't forget the golden rule of child rearing in Australia: you're best not to teach kids too much as that might give them an unfair advantage over others.

The seven ages of man

I grew up with the traditional knowledge that man's life consisted of seven ages: infancy, childhood, adolescence, adulthood, middle age, old age and dotage. It came as a surprise, therefore, to find that in Australia the seven ages of man consist only of two: those under 25 and those past it.

Up to the age of 25, being an Australian involves a lot of hard work.

Men must sport an all-year-round suntan, wear zinc cream on their noses and maintain a general air of inhibited aggression. Women must keep up with fashions, brush their teeth four or five times a day, and find a place to go to every night irrespective of climatic (or climactic) conditions.

After 25 come the good times.

Now you can really let yourself go. This is a chance for the ladies to spend entire seasons in Target tentfrocks and Carmen heated rollers, perched on Keith Lord kitchen stools. For gentlemen it's an opportunity to let their stomachs hang over those tight King Gee shorts and play with their Taiwanese thongs while reminiscing with friends.

Everyone can relax now.

Most importantly, stay exclusively within your own age group. After two centuries of experimentation, Australians have found that knocking around only with one's contemporaries is the perfect way to age badly without ever really noticing it.

This way of all going down-the-hill together is Australia's answer to the secret of eternal youth.

Before 25

After 25

The bedroom

A poet once called the eyes "the mirrors of the soul". Evidently he wasn't Australian. Australians learn early from their parents that the real mirror of the soul is the state of one's bedroom.

They learn that the more unused and deserted a bedroom appears, the better impression its owners will make on the world. The bedrooms Australians admire the most, in fact, are those which look as if their occupants slept elsewhere.

To create an environment, therefore, where your partner or occasional visitor will feel comfortable, you must put all old-fashioned notions of decorating aside and take as your inspiration — the motel room.

Go for the unlived-in look. Keep everything out of sight. A bedroom should never be tainted by the identity of those inhabiting it. This is a courteous society and it is bad manners to have a personality of one's own.

Things private must be safely stowed away. It's best to give bedrooms a rigid and uninviting appearance. Eradicate any hint of their real purpose. Make sure beds are all made up by 7 am to discourage those who might want to use them again.

The loungeroom

A well-designed home in Australia ought to be able to trap any would-be visitors at the front door, and then keep them there for as long as possible or until they decide to go away.

Any soundly built house must also be able to encourage relatives, and especially friends, to enter through the back door so that they may get ensnared in the kitchen. This is where most social activities occur.

The loungeroom is the last place you take people into.

Unfortunately, there *are* rare occasions when you're forced to use the loungeroom. Here are a few handy hints to ensure that the guests' sojourn there is of minimum length:

1 Ensure the loungeroom has a stale ambience so guests won't want to stay.

2 Loungeroom furniture ought to appear cemented in or bolted down. Create the impression that should any item be moved a centimetre either way, the owners would feel incredible personal distress.

3 Push sofas, chairs and settees against the walls so that visitors have to sit a long way from each other. This prevents any undue intimacy and discourages relaxing.

4 Place coffee tables either too close to allow people to stretch out their legs or otherwise just out of reach.

5 Leave huge empty spaces in the middle of the room. This facilitates vacuuming and also reproduces the perimetric life-style of the Australian continent.

The twilight zone

Old people in Greece or the Middle East are always expected to live in the same house with their sons and daughters. There they are continually subjected to various pressures like having to cope with boisterous grandchildren who not only expect the poor aged folk to amuse and entertain them, but also ask innumerable painful questions about the past, lost youth or dead friends.

In the Caucasus or Spain, the elderly are even expected to work up to twelve hours a day, well into their late eighties. Trudging up and down hills, shuffling in and out of vineyards and farmyards, forced in the evenings to preside over long dinners with large demanding families who perennially expect help or advice, the old people in these countries just know no rest.

Here in Australia the elderly are dealt with in a much more humane way. Australia, being a modern and progressive society, aims to provide those in their twilight years with a calm, worry-free existence. For this reason steps are taken from the outset to protect the aged from any possible abuse or exploitation by their families.

Following years of study and experience, it has been discovered that the best way to achieve this is to gather the elderly together and keep them safely (and securely) ensconced in one place, under the care of strangers.

Amazingly enough, the best environment for this purpose has been found to be an institution known as

"Ah, come on, Mum and Dad, it's only for the next twenty or thirty years!"

the Nursing Home*. Often built in the grounds of an abandoned mansion, such a home-away-from-home usually consists of many small rooms (not all of them in need of a coat of paint), one large verandah or sunroom with two or three TV sets and corridors just wide enough to permit the free flow of wheelchairs.

The Nursing Home's advantages are obvious. Here the elderly:

- can look forward to peaceful medicated sleep without the danger of being woken early by kids running around the house

- don't have to suffer the stresses of a generation gap since they are exclusively with people of their own age group

- don't have to answer questions

- are away from the prying eyes of a cruel young world

- may spend their final twenty or thirty years in unhurried serenity and without any stimuli whatever.

After a certain point you have to start getting your parents used to the idea of spending their remaining decades in such a dignified environment. *The general idea is to explain that you are sending them to a place where you will be out of their hair.*

Explain clearly and authoritatively that here you will not cause them any more problems than they already have. It's also a good idea to embark on their re-education programmes well in advance, and the following pointers should help:

1 From about 40 onwards, encourage parents to cut down on mixing with younger people. They should start attending bingo nights or lawn bowls instead.

A name often changed by deed poll to "Retirement Village"

71

2 Strongly discourage them from spending time at your place. Point out what fun they could have in an environment exclusively of their own generation.

3 Visit them at fewer and fewer intervals so that eventually, except for a couple of hours on Christmas Day, they won't ever have to see their family again.

Renovations

Most renovations in Australia begin innocuously enough. The home, no matter how lovely, comfortable or expensive, suddenly proves inadequate for living in. If only there were a small door here, a wider window there, a kitchen sink on the opposite wall and slate tiles in the bathroom — if only these things were done, then the home would surely be perfect.

But sadly, irrespective of where you put the new patio, sink, toilet bowl, spare room or open fire-place, someone (spouse, relatives or friends) will explain to you most patiently that these things should not have been placed *there*. On the roof, yes, in the backyard maybe, or hanging above the front gate; anywhere, in fact, but not where *you* had decided to place them.

Events now get out of control. The renovations soon spread to the entire household and take over large chunks of the people's lives.

There's cement in the carpets, paint marks on the curtains, tacks and nails between sofa cushions, sudden cracks above the staircase, nastily scratched window panes, bits missing out of doorways, permanently grubby taps, mysteriously broken vases, chandeliers hanging by single threads of wire, laundries filled with rubble, garden-beds smothered by bricks, corridors that become impassable for months.

Could all this chaos be accidental?

Far from being haphazard, renovations in Australia follow a clear and traceable pattern. Research has shown that each stage of a renovation bears, in fact, a strong correlation to the marital problems of those undertaking it:

ADDITIONAL STOREY TO SUBURBAN HOME	Couple would prefer divorce but can't afford it
BACKYARD SHED TURNED INTO DEN	Husband caught up in mid-life crisis but too afraid to have outside liaisons
EXTENDING THE LOUNGEROOM	Wife trying to keep husband suspected of having affairs at home
SEPARATE DINING AREA CREATED	Marriage in socio-economic rut, wife dreams of mixing with people above her station
NEW BATHROOM	Husband dissatisfied with sex-life; wife approaching menopause
NEW KITCHEN AND BUILT-INS	Marriage on the rocks — wife threatens to walk out
MODERNIZING NARROW WINDOWS	Spouses fancy some infidelity but haven't found right person
WHOLE HOUSE REDECORATED	Couples have simply given up on each other and lead separate lives

Be warned, however. If you wish to keep the marriage going, do not complete renovations. Leave bits of construction work permanently unfinished. It may be anything from a few missing tiles under the sink to a huge gap in the back wall.

In Australia experience has shown that once renovations are completed, and there are no other possible improvements to be made, the property somehow always ends up being sold.

Keeping the peace

Overburdened perhaps with the drudgery of house-work, mothers in Europe often allow their families to get out of control. Husbands, children, relatives are all permitted to go about unchecked as they give free vent to their egos. The result is heated arguments, noisy exchanges and extended family discussions on every imaginable topic. Brought up in such a bellicose environment, young Europeans soon become outspoken, and confident, with strong personalities of their own.

Australian mothers would never permit such lawlessness.

An Australian mother knows only too well that the family is a volatile institution upon whose unruly members she must exercise a steadying influence. She also knows it is up to her to be peacekeeper if they are not to plunge into anarchy and barbarism through the unchecked and dangerous practices of open argument, face-to-face conflict and general discussion of ideas, subversive to the welfare of the clan.

The process of *keeping the peace* within the clan is a difficult operation and any woman with plans to start a family will have to learn to perform several complicated manouvres worthy of a seasoned diplomat:

1 To run the family properly along Australian lines, your first task must be to keep the various family members, i.e. sons, daughters, spouse, etc., as far apart from each other as possible, so that not even a hint of

conflict may ensue between them. Lines towards this end are:

"Don't bother your father."

"Leave the kids alone."

"You better tell me first."

"You're upsetting your sister."

"No arguing in this house now."

You will have to do this from early childhood on, otherwise some deep attachments could appear which, later on, might lead to all kinds of complications.

2 The job of the peacekeeper is not only to ascertain that family members don't get close enough to one another to have any kind of contact, but also to ensure that if, by chance, trouble *does* ensue, it doesn't ever get resolved. Such resolutions, after all, could lead everyone into uncharted territory.

"Stop it both of you!"

"I don't want to hear any more about it!"

"I think you two better stay away from each other."

The advantage of unresolved conflicts is to ensure that generations of good Australians grow up without knowing how to argue and then make up. This intransigent attitude has also the added advantage of training everyone to live with a general sense of unease and tension from childhood on.

3 Your ultimate aim will be to discourage any kind of exchange of views, whether personal or general, since all such exchanges can potentially lead to a full-blown drama. Even though the family insist that it's only a game that they play, you never know, things can get out of hand.

A family at peace.

The reaction to any healthy European-style argument should always be:

"Oh my God, the family's falling apart!"

"I knew it would come to this."

"What am I going to do now?"

"Why can't we just have peace?"

Do not be discouraged by the difficulties you might encounter. With practice the deft hand of the manipulator will become undetectable and you'll be able to work miracles for years to come without ever being sprung.

How to recognize your father

The Australian family is run strictly along British parliamentary lines.

Father is like the country's Governor-General. Hardly recognizable except for his uniform, and seen only at special celebrations, he makes long-winded speeches which he knows are not going to make an iota of difference.

Mother operates like a modern Prime Minister. Expected to make important unpopular decisions but always promising to review the situation at a later date, she tries to remain in power for as long as possible.

Children represent the Opposition. Heard only after much whingeing, shouting and stamping of feet, they feel permanently frustrated and are critical of all family decisions as a matter of course.

Thus, on most days, one may see *mother* taunted by the Opposition across the kitchen table, or the Prime Minister cajoling *father* into signing any number of bills, while on rare occasions *children* might even get to hold the Governor-General's hand.

All patriotic Australians abide by these roles, knowing that attempts to trespass them could plunge the whole family unit into a constitutional crisis.

How to be no trouble

The most important attribute of any child in Australia. Don't get confused by overseas notions that children must actually do something for their parents to be proud of them. In Australia the highest praise you can give any youngster is to deem it *no trouble*. This must be pointed out at every opportunity.

For Good Children

"Oh, Kim's never any problem."

"Aren't you lucky!"

"You'd hardly know Kerry was there."

"Oh, isn't that nice."

"We certainly don't hear a peep out of Ronnie."

"Wonderful!"

"And Tom's a perfect angel."

"I don't know how you do it."

Conversely, you must always point out how much trouble your neighbours, or cousins, or sisters are having with their particular brood.

For Bad Children

"Her Robyn's forever making a racket at the piano."

"Isn't that awful!"

"The flat's always messed up with Dana's chemistry set."

"Oh dear, how dangerous!"

"I don't know how they put up with Lynn's singing."

"Must be dreadful."

"Oh, Kenny's a perfect angel, he's no trouble at all!"

"And then there's Ricky who never stops asking questions about the family."

"It just goes to show..."

Overseas parents are forever talking about their children's peculiar ambitions and about how much they have to do to turn the kids into computer geniuses, concert pianists and champion gymnasts. Australian parents, level-headed and naturally modest folk, feel a strong distaste for this kind of overt behaviour and simply will not be part of any such pushiness and presumption.

After all, children may have their own personalities, they may even have special talents, but they shouldn't be allowed to exercise them at the expense of everyone else.

Several years ago, when I was still new to Australia's ways, I was told by a couple at a party: "Oh, we are very proud of our children, they're no trouble at all."

My immediate reaction was to congratulate them. I imagined a pair of brilliant young musicians practising all day long with the encouragement of their parents, or better even, two young electronics wizards preparing themselves for the 21st century.

It was not for some time that I learnt the true meaning of those words. The description of the children as "no trouble" simply meant that the kids:

(a) didn't do anything in particular;

(b) stayed out of their parents' hair;

(c) never spoke unless they were spoken to;

(d) spent a lot of time out of the home in pinball palours; and

(e) in the evenings sat around for hours staring into thin TV.

Father's Day

Being a father involves much the same liabilities all over the world. To be woken by a crying baby in a hut on the Congo is no more romantic than coping with a houseful of screaming infants in Canberra. Waiting up for a teenage daughter till 2 am is equally anxiety provoking in Melbourne and Montevideo. Scraping together enough to pay for the children's tuition carries about the same emotional gratification in Atlantic City as in Adelaide.

But being a father in Australia does present a number of extra responsibilities and duties not found on other parts of the globe, obligations which all Australian fathers have to remember.

Firstly, it's wise when bringing up children in Australia to discourage them from wanting to communicate with you. Ensure that the kids give you a wide berth at all times. Most Australian dads have realized for some time now that the best way to foster their children's development is not to talk to them at all. Difficult as this may seem to practise, you must realize that it is for the good of the kids if the contact between them and yourself is reduced to an absolute minimum. The advantages are obvious:

(a) You won't make any mistakes in their education.

(b) There won't be any dependency on each other.

Father's Day Armistice.

(c) Children will eventually learn to become like gum-trees on the edge of a desert — self-reliant and isolated.

As an Australian father you are in a difficult position. You must sire your children and then never put in any further effort in case you confuse them. In fact, Australian fatherhood should be effortless. Sort of like weed-free gardening.

Make liberal use of the back-up services at your disposal and leave the moulding of the children entirely to:

- their mother

- their school-teachers

- the occasional child-welfare officer

- the manager of the local pin-ball parlour

It's important that you should also breed tension in the children because it will help them cope with friends, colleagues and employers later on in life. Here are a few simple techniques to help you maintain the optimum level of tension all year round:

(a) Should the children want something, you must automatically say "no" then walk out of the room.

(b) No matter what, always look at them disapprovingly, as if they had done something wrong.

(c) Never make it clear to anybody whether or not you are angry, upset, pleased or hurt by what they've done.

Naturally, even with a lot of antipodean restraint, things that need to be said between a father and his kids accumulate over the course of time. For this purpose Father's Day was designated as a special day in the

Australian calendar.

On Father's Day, after a year of distant glaring, you are permitted at last to talk to the children. You may now shake hands, accept gifts and, in the presence of witnesses, converse freely about accumulated concerns.

"How's it going?"

"Good, Dad."

"Everything OK?"

"Oh, yeah."

"That's all right then."

Remember, though. The rest of the year you must remain a silent enigma.

Growing up normal

Since Australia is a land of the future, great emphasis is placed upon the young. In the worn-out, tired societies of Europe, children are merely forced to conform with established patterns. Here all patterns have been dispensed with. Now you have a chance to grow up freely and be yourself, provided you take note of a few simple hints.

1 Make sure you get paid for even the tiniest bit of work you may do for your parents. Grumble about the money they give you. Irrespective of the amount, always demand more. This way you'll get an early understanding of the wage arbitration system.

2 There must be tension between yourself and the rest of the family at all times. The slightest request from parents must produce irritation. Ensure they comprehend that everything you do for them is a real effort.

3 Never show enthusiasm. People might misunderstand and think that you're drunk or on drugs. Besides, you'll save heaps of energy. If you must be enthusiastic about something, it should always be about your *own* plans, projects or ideas, because in Australia this is what "enthusiasm" is usually taken to mean.

*"Look, Dad, we've told you — it's 7 bucks
for a wax'n polish and 4 for the tyre black."*

4 At school never act too intelligent as that will single you out. If you happen to know the answer to a question, best to keep quiet about it so dumber friends won't think that there is something funny about you.

5 Make your elders happy by not having a point of view of your own. Most Australian grown-ups don't like contradiction. Just repeat what they want to hear and they'll be very grateful to you. Refrain from making any decisions yourself. Ideal types of conversation with adults ought to be:
   "Do you want lunch?"
   "If you like."
   "How hungry are you?"
   "I'm not sure."

6 The last people in the world you should tell your problems to are your father and mother because they already have plenty of worries as things are. It's bad enough that you were born so young and with so little sympathy for their situation, you shouldn't have to trouble them as well.

7 Don't ever expect your family to be one hundred percent behind you because that is not the Australian way. When your parents take the side of teachers, friends, relatives or the police against you, they are simply preparing you for the hardships of the real world ahead.

How to say "No" to everything

You must learn to be against everything, because that is terribly Australian. All modern-thinking progressive Australians are opposed to change or anything new and are respected for it.

In fact, more Australians have put their names to petitions that were *against* new projects, developments, schemes or proposals than *for* them.

Occasionally there's trouble with overseas investors, bankers and architects who don't seem to understand that in Australia it is normal to be against: tall buildings, long bridges, tunnels, airplanes, airports, heliports, imports, exports, holiday resorts, strikes, strike-breakers, smoking, non-smoking, lopping down trees, putting up sports grounds, digging into the earth, damming up water, medical experiments, slow reactors, fast railways and modern inventions, since it shows that you are a serious person with deep committed feelings.

The fact that the country might go to pot as a result is simply irrelevant.

An advanced party of Australian Citizens Against Everything

How to start a rumour

In Moscow or Paris, no sooner does a political event take place than some local humourist has made up an elaborate story about it. When Ronald Reagan met Mikhail Gorbachev in 1986, for instance, they'd come up with this sort of thing.

> *The American president asked his Russian counterpart if there was anything he wanted from the States. Yes, said Gorbachev, I want to make love to the stunning star of television's "Dynasty", Linda Evans. Reagan came back the next day and said: I spoke to Miss Evans and she'll go to Moscow only on the condition that you open the Soviet borders and give everyone their freedom. Gorbachev's face lit up. Ah, he said, then she must really love me. She wants the two of us to be left all alone!*

In Australia events are treated rather differently.

When a friend arrived from Paris a few years ago, on a lecture tour on the French political situation, after a particularly serious and involved session he expected his listeners to ask, "What then is the French Government's position on atomic testing?" Instead they took him aside and said:

"Tell us, is it true that the French President's really a transvestite?"

While other nations have their humourists, Australia

"Heard any good rumours about me lately?"

has rumourists instead. One might say Australians have a great sense of rumour*.

If some upstart politician gets into office, in Europe people would say "He's an incompetent fool who'll soon have his comeuppance". In Australia, however, no one would dare predict a career cut short by mere incompetence. Australians might remark instead:

"Of course the gambling debts had to be paid"

"Must be someone's crony"; or,

"I wonder if he's still trading in drugs?"

British legal and constitutional brains have battled for centuries to come up with the concept of "innocent unless proven guilty". Likewise Australian pundits have created an equally effective formula regarding the rights of citizens, namely *If it's rumoured, it must be true.*

Particularly effective rumours when casually stated are those which feature: busted marriages, suicide attempts, drug dependancies, underworld connections, ruptured colons.

If you become a public figure in Australia it is normal that there should be rumours surrounding you. In fact, the mark of fame is whether or not your very own rumours are spread. While showing great disgust and shock at the obviously untrue allegations regarding yourself, however, you must at the same time play fair and:

(a) be the first to believe every possible vicious rumour spread about others;

(b) pass on these rumours yourself, else you might break the chain and throw the country into confusion.

The Australian love of rumour seems to originate in the family. As parents won't talk much about their true past, and kids won't talk about where they go once they're out of the house, it follows that everyone has to rely on hearsay and conjecture to get at the truth. And they do.

Remember, in Australia you may say anything, as long as you don't back it up with facts.

The best way to introduce a good Australian rumour is without a single change in intonation and with one of the following lines:
"That's not what I heard..."
"I wonder how many people realize..."
"My lawyer told me different..."
Since every Australian is at heart a rumourist, they will find this irresistible.

ROBERT TREBORLANG

Born in ... grown up in ... educated at ... Robert Treborlang is admirably qualified to write on the problems of being normal in Australia. He understands the principles of passivity, is highly apologetic, never causes any trouble and works closely with his wife Moi Moi who is many years younger than him but not as photogenic. An earlier book, "How to Survive Australia" was a runaway best-seller.

MARK KNIGHT

Mark Knight . . . political cartoonist, has commented on subjects from the Australian economy to the personalities of politicians in the national press. He owes his success to his mother who saw enough potential in his early scribblings to take them to a newspaper editor. Born in Marrickville, New South Wales, he is eminently qualified to pictorialize the Australian psyche.